# Letter to a Dandelion
*Earth Verse for Gardeners & Nature Lovers*

## *Praise for Letter to a Dandelion*

⚡ "Glover's charming collection ... celebrates ... humanity's relationship to nature within the context of gardening and stewardship.... Blending the reverent and the playful ... key lines achieve a sophistication, grace, and insight.... In 'The Gift,' one of the best in his collection, Glover quietly meditates on the universe: ... 'from galaxies to layered rose.'"– **Booklife Reviews**

★★★★★ "*Letter to a Dandelion: Earth Verse for Gardeners & Nature Lovers* ... is a true wonder of beauty, hope, humor, peace, and simplicity ... an extraordinary read! ... I love this poetry! I read this collection 'with pleasure at my leisure.' I warmly recommend this gem of a book!" —M. Fasquel, **Readers' Favorite**

"Glover employs rhymes ... astutely and finely rendered to demonstrate literary prowess.... Libraries seeking contemporary nature-oriented poetry ... will especially welcome the opportunity to add *Letter to a Dandelion* to their collections.... readers ... will find ... a perfect key for enjoying and celebrating both the outdoors and literary talent." —D. Donovan, Senior Reviewer, **Midwest Book Review**

## *Praise for Jeffry Glover's Books*

★★★★★ "...*The Wildebeest and a Bunch of Crock and Other Animal Story Poems* is a delightful compilation.... The standout element of the book is its inventive storytelling ... demonstrating Glover's mastery of wordplay and imagery ... a treasure trove of literary enjoyment ... a must-have ... perfect for reading aloud at home or in the classroom." —C. Thompson, **Readers' Favorite**

"Jeffry Glover's delightful creation ... will translate to hours of fun and interactive pleasure, while libraries that choose *The Wildebeest and a Bunch of Crock and Other Animal Story Poems* for its solid verse and appealing cover will find its underlying value lends to greater appreciation of nature...." —D. Donovan, Senior Reviewer, **Midwest Book Review**

★★★★★ *9 Lively Cat Tales and Other Pet Poems* is quite simply pure fun.... The poems and stories are ... delightfully purrfect." —E. Hills Orford, **Readers' Favorite**

*9 Lively Cat Tales and Other Pet Poems* : "While he admits to drawing inspiration from many sources, such as William Blake and Edward Lear, ... this reviewer would like to add Ogden Nash to the list since Glover has a way of ... weaving in fabricated words as well as the element of surprise.... Quill says: An enjoyable read from end to end." —A. Lock, **Feathered Quill**

To find more books by Jeffry Glover, please visit PoetryPie.com.

# Letter to a Dandelion
*Earth Verse for Gardeners & Nature Lovers*

Jeffry Glover

POEMS FOR PLEASURE PRESS
Stoughton, Wisconsin

Copyright 2025 Jeffry Glover. All rights reserved. No part of this work may be reproduced, transmitted, or distributed by any means, electronic or mechanical, without express written permission of the author except for brief excerpts, which may be quoted in reviews. For permission to use material from this book please contact the publisher.

Published by Poems for Pleasure Press LLC
contact@poemsforpleasurepress.com
Stoughton, Wisconsin, United States of America
Order books online at www.PoemsforPleasurePress.com

Publisher's Cataloging-in-Publication
(Provided by Cassidy Cataloguing Services, Inc.)

| | |
|---|---|
| Names: | Glover, Jeffry (Jeffry Keith), 1946- author. \| Bausman, Mary, cover designer. |
| Title: | Letter to a dandelion : Earth verse for gardeners & nature lovers / Jeffry Glover ; [cover by Mary Bausman]. |
| Description: | First edition. \| Stoughton, Wisconsin : Poems for Pleasure Press, 2025. \| Interest age level: 12 and up. |
| Identifiers: | ISBN: 978-1948854078 (hardcover) \| 978-1948854085 (softcover) \| 978-1948854092 (ebook-ePub) \| LCCN: 2024925257 |
| Subjects: | LCSH: Gardens--Poetry. \| Nature--Poetry. \| Animals--Poetry. \| LCGFT: Nature poetry. \| Humorous poetry. \| Stories in rhyme. \| BISAC: HUMOR / Form / Limericks & Verse. \| POETRY / Subjects & Themes / Animals & Nature. \| NATURE / Plants / General |
| Classification: | LCC: PS3607.L6844 L48 2025 \| DDC: 811/.6--dc23 |

Library of Congress Control Number: 2024925257

Grateful acknowledgement for the cover design by Mary Bausman, layout by KJ Forest, and PCIP by Cassidy Cataloguing Services. The author draws inspiration from many sources including Untermeyer's "Long Feud," Wordsworth's "I Wandered Lonely as a Cloud," and Walt Whitman's "Leaves of Grass." "The Dandelion's Reply" stems from "Dandelions," *Green Immigrants, The Plants That Transformed America*, by Claire Shaver Haughton, Harcourt, Brace, Jovanovich, NY, 1980. Fonts by: ©2010 The Crimson Text Project Authors (github.com/googlefonts/Crimson), ©2018 The Crimson Pro Project Authors (github.com/Fonthausen/CrimsonPro), and ©2016 The Nunito Sans Project Authors (github.com/Fonthausen/NunitoSans), with SIL Open Font License version 1.1 viewable at https://scripts.sil.org/OFL. Author photo by Express Portraits. To support sustainability our books are printed-on-demand by Ingram Content Group on responsibly sourced, archival quality paper (www.ingramspark.com/environmental-responsibility)

First Edition 2025

Printed in the United States of America

# Contents

Introduction ........................................................................................ 1
   Welcome to Our Yard and Garden ................................................ 2
I. Welcome Spring ............................................................................. 3
   Exit Winter, Enter Spring ............................................................... 4
   First Day of Spring ......................................................................... 5
   April's Coming ................................................................................ 6
   Daffodil Delights ............................................................................. 7
   Full Spring Ahead .......................................................................... 8
   Birdsong ......................................................................................... 10
   Apple Blossoms ............................................................................ 11
   Blooms and Bees .......................................................................... 12
   May ................................................................................................ 13
   Falling Apple Blossoms ............................................................... 14
   Magnolias in the Daylight ........................................................... 15
   Lilies of the Valley ........................................................................ 16
   When Zephyrs Whoosh and Blow ............................................. 17
   An Evening Still and Fair ............................................................ 18
   The Midnight Moon .................................................................... 19
II. Garden Time ................................................................................ 21
   A Garden of Verses ..................................................................... 22
   Morning in the Garden ............................................................... 23
   Garden Glory ................................................................................ 24
   From Seed to Harvest .................................................................. 25
   Delicious Discovery ..................................................................... 26
   Ripe Strawberries ......................................................................... 27
   Our Plastic Garden Owl .............................................................. 28
   Garden Instructions ..................................................................... 29

    Weeding Time ............................................................... 30
    The Hoe, My Woe ......................................................... 31
    Rompin' Rabbits ............................................................ 32
    Bunny Defense .............................................................. 33
    My Groundhog .............................................................. 34
    Windy Day ..................................................................... 35
    Yard Work ..................................................................... 36
    Rainy Morning .............................................................. 37
    Storm Brings Green ...................................................... 38
III. When Mowing Harkens .................................................. 39
    Dew, Adieu ................................................................... 40
    Mowing At Leisure ........................................................ 41
    When Mowing Harkens ................................................ 42
    The Visitor ..................................................................... 43
    Trim Grass ..................................................................... 44
    Grass Too Long ............................................................. 45
    Kicking Grass ................................................................ 46
    A Lawn Going to Weeds .............................................. 48
IV. Letter To a Dandelion .................................................... 51
    Dandelions Like Stars .................................................... 52
    Dandelions Like Grass .................................................. 53
    Letter to a Dandelion .................................................... 54
    The Dandelion's Reply .................................................. 55
    Apology Letter to a Dandelion ..................................... 58
    Summer Weeds ............................................................. 59
    Confronting Creeping Charlie ...................................... 62
    Weeds We Inherit ......................................................... 64
    Buckthorn Trees ........................................................... 65
    Crabgrass ....................................................................... 66
V. Flights of Summer ............................................................ 67

| | |
|---|---|
| Sunrise | 68 |
| Morning | 69 |
| Robin's Reveille | 70 |
| Birds of Summer | 71 |
| Our Bird Feeders | 72 |
| Birdie at Our Feeder | 73 |
| The Baltimore Oriole | 74 |
| Our Baltimore Orioles | 75 |
| The Joy of Hummingbirds | 76 |
| A Blue Jay's Intentions | 77 |
| Dawn Visit | 78 |
| One Summer Day | 79 |
| Butterfly Wings | 80 |
| Majestic Monarch | 81 |
| The Dainty Moth | 82 |
| To a Tree | 83 |
| Renditions of the Wren | 84 |
| VI. Golden Days of Summer | 85 |
| Morning Sun | 86 |
| Crystal Rainbow Morning | 87 |
| Morning Glory Story | 88 |
| Summer Iris | 89 |
| Bushes Blocking Windows | 90 |
| The Thrush | 91 |
| Silver Maple Seeds | 92 |
| The Tree Next Door | 93 |
| Watching Squirrels | 94 |
| Squirrel Story | 95 |
| Dragonfly Engineering | 96 |
| Chipmunks | 97 |

    Verdant Moss .................................................................. 98
    A Tree and Me ............................................................... 99
    Sun Day ........................................................................ 100
    Sun Setting .................................................................. 101
    Storm Clouds .............................................................. 102
    Lightning Show ........................................................... 103
    Afternoon Storm ......................................................... 104
    The Rainbow Road ..................................................... 105

VII. Day and Night on the River ........................................ 107
    Adorning Morning ...................................................... 108
    Birds Awake ................................................................. 109
    The Lolling Lily .......................................................... 110
    Passing Swans ............................................................. 111
    The River Wide .......................................................... 112
    River Light .................................................................. 113
    A Clangor of Cranes ................................................... 114
    Geese Return ............................................................... 115
    Evening Magic ............................................................ 116
    Night on the River ..................................................... 117
    Captivating Crickets .................................................. 118
    The Gibbous Moon .................................................... 119
    In the Dot-to-Dot Sky ................................................ 120

VIII. Leaves on Grass ........................................................... 121
    Inklings of Fall ............................................................ 122
    When Fall Has Come ................................................. 123
    Fall's Grandeur ............................................................ 124
    Cruising Leaves ........................................................... 125
    When Leaves Let Go .................................................. 126
    Racing with Leaves ..................................................... 127
    Leaves and More Leaves ............................................. 128

    Leaf Exercise ............................................................. 129
    Snake Escape ............................................................ 130
    Deck Leaves .............................................................. 131
    Leaves Keep Falling .................................................. 132
    Leaves Gone But Not For Long ............................... 133
    Time To Leave .......................................................... 134
    Oak Leaves Hold On ............................................... 136
IX. Autumn Time ............................................................ 137
    Hummers Gone South ............................................ 138
    Garden Harvest ....................................................... 139
    Cold and Rainy Weather ........................................ 140
    Orange Twilight ....................................................... 141
    One Fall Night .......................................................... 142
    Harvest Moon .......................................................... 143
    Time for Planting Tulips ......................................... 144
    Goose Summer Gone .............................................. 145
    Geese Migration ...................................................... 146
    Cardinal Plans ......................................................... 147
    Hints of Winter ........................................................ 148
    How Autumn Leaves .............................................. 149
X. Winter Wonders ......................................................... 151
    Before the Snow ...................................................... 152
    First Snow ................................................................ 153
    Snowflakes Dancing ............................................... 155
    No Snow Woe .......................................................... 156
    Winter Weather ....................................................... 157
    At 10 Below .............................................................. 158
    River Ice ................................................................... 159
    Not Too Cold ........................................................... 160
    On Our Snowy Street ............................................. 161

Plow's Been Through ............................................................. 162
  Leaves Waft and Wander ...................................................... 163
  Snowy Day ............................................................................ 164
  Squirrel Tracks in Snow ........................................................ 166
  Meditation on Snow .............................................................. 167
  Snowy Magic ........................................................................ 168
  Winter Morning .................................................................... 170
XI. Winter Into Spring Again ..................................................... 171
  Waiting Out Winter .............................................................. 172
  Bird Tracks ........................................................................... 173
  Think Summer! ..................................................................... 174
  Glistening Branches .............................................................. 175
  The Sun Is Beaming .............................................................. 176
  Melting Snowman ................................................................. 177
  Warmer Days Ahead ............................................................. 178
  The Quiet Crocus .................................................................. 179
  Leaf Gathering ...................................................................... 180
  The Gift ................................................................................ 181
  Waiting for Daffodils ............................................................ 182
  Spring Morning .................................................................... 183
XII. The March of Time ............................................................. 185
  The March of Time ............................................................... 187
About the Author ........................................................................ 189

x

# Introduction

Dear Reader,

Letter to a Dandelion—Earth Verse for Gardeners & Nature Lovers is filled with light-hearted rhyming poems to take you on an amusing trek around an imaginary yard and garden through the seasons of the year. Experience the wonders of spring flowers in bloom, summer birds in flight, colorful autumn leaves, and the first snowflakes of winter, along with the challenges of mowing grass, raking leaves, pulling weeds (especially dandelions), and fending off hungry rabbits in the garden! In addition to the title poem, favorite poems include "Morning Sun," "Night on the River," "Captivating Crickets," "Rainbow Road," "The Gift," and more—over 150 poems in all.

I wish to acknowledge those who have graciously assisted me in producing this book at Poems for Pleasure Press, and all who have offered support and assistance along the way. My readers make writing my books of verse worthwhile and a pleasure. Thank you.

For more fun read-aloud poetry books, visit my website at www.JeffryGlover.com. Enjoy!

## Welcome to Our Yard and Garden

Read with pleasure
At your leisure
About our yard and
Lovely garden
Through each season
Warm to freezin':
Springtime growing,
Summer mowing,
Fall leaves blowing,
Winter snowing,
Watching nature
Do her thing
All year round
And back to spring!

# I. Welcome Spring

## Exit Winter, Enter Spring

Old Man Winter tipped his hat,
Said, "Goodbye, cold, enough of that,"
Left the house where he had been
With door ajar, when Spring walked in
Exclaiming, "This place will not do.
Let's freshen it with something new,
A different color is what I mean;
I plan to paint this whole house green!
And as for the windows, tinged with gray,
I'm going to wash them right away.
In fact, this place needs lightening up,
These cloudy curtains aren't bright enough."
So with her sun participating,
Spring went to work redecorating.

## First Day of Spring

Spring is here today at last,
Winter weather newly past;
With longer daylight sun supplies
Temperatures are on the rise.
Finally gone are ice and snow,
Tulip buds begin to show,
And geese excited congregate
On the lake to celebrate.
Squirrels are foraging about;
Robins will be next, no doubt.
Dormant grass, still brown, is seen
Impatient to turn emerald green.
Soon will follow clouds and rain.
Hail, fair spring! We won't complain!

## April's Coming

April's coming once again;
March is marching past.
Cloudy days bring ample rain
And daylength's gaining fast.
Spring announces warmth will come
With freezing nights soon gone.
Daffodils have just begun
To show and grace the lawn.
Zephyrs through the light spring air
Are sporting whimsy now.
Days are varied, full of flair
As temperatures allow.
It is a season made for hope
With flowers, a kaleidoscope.

## Daffodil Delights

New beauty bringing to the earth,
Daffodils say spring!
Beaming bright for all they're worth;
If flowers could, they'd sing

As they seem to dance about
Waltzing in the wind,
Then curtsy when they're out of breath
 So low their stems may bend.

We do not pick them when we see
Their lively vivid hue;
We'd rather see them growing free
The way wild flowers do.

Their fragrance lends a faint bouquet
That's truly heaven sent
To give the air a rare perfume
Lightly evident.

They stay a week or two at most
Then slowly fade away;
Yet while they're here they bring us cheer
Returning every May.

-----------------
With a nod to Wordsworth's "I Wandered Lonely as a Cloud" and Glover's "Wordsworth's Solitude" in *Poetry Pie, Volume 1*.

## Full Spring Ahead

Earth enjoys sun's warming spring
When winter snow has gone.
Early birds are heard to sing
In trees around the lawn.

For many days the rains will come
To waken sleeping grass,
Soak and sink into the sod,
Then clouds and storms will pass.

All around are signs of green,
Crocus pushing out,
Daffodils are rising up,
Next tulips round about.

Blossoms bloom with colors bright:
Pinks, purples, yellows, reds
Will open under warm sunlight
In bonnie flower beds.

Birds returning mate and nest;
Frogs begin their croaks.
Swans are swimming on the lake
With graceful steady strokes.

It is the season of renewal;
Growth shows everywhere.
Life abundantly returns
On earth fresh, green, and fair.

Tendrils coiled on lattices
Hold up the morning glory;
Hummingbirds arrive to feed
Quick-sipping, transitory.

Little breezes cross the lake
Waving as they come,
Flitting here and everywhere,
No sooner there than done.

Squirrels abound and hop about
Searching for a cache,
Chase each other, flit their tails,
Frisky as they dash.

Robins dig for juicy worms,
Hunting never done,
Listening with heads side-cocked,
A working marathon.

Fish are jumping just for joy
In the swim of things.
These and many wonders more
Are all announcing spring!

## Birdsong

A cheerful song one day I heard—
The chirping of a little bird.
I listened as it seemed to say,
"How wonderful I'm here today,
Happy, healthy and can fly
Near the ground or way up high.
And when I want then I will perch
On an oak branch or a birch,
Find good food, all I need,
Be it worm or ripened seed.
Nature's generosity
Daily does provide for me.
This is why I'm happy here
Nine months out of every year."

## Apple Blossoms

I'm waiting, watching patiently
The springtime flowering of a tree,
An apple tree specifically,
Buds opening spectacularly.
Is there a better thing to do?
Oh, yes, I could be working, true,
But what's more worthwhile than to see
Nature in its finery
Turning buds into bright blossoms,
Bursting forth in colors awesome?
I like to stop sometimes and look
And consider how it took
Ten million years or more for this,
A splendid sight that's not to miss.

## Blooms and Bees

Blooms and bees on flowered trees
Bring spring unto its own.
Sun vies with freeze, and zephyr breeze
Fluffs clouds like feathers blown.
Bright daffodils dance for our eyes
And bend when winds blow brisk.
Tall tulips rise of such a size
Their colors can't be missed.
The very air seems happy where
It chases 'round the ground.
Faint fragrances tempt bees to care
Where pollen can be found.
It is a time when spring is dressed
In brand new clothes of nature's best.

## May

My calendar at last says May
And so it is outside today!
Trees are flowering bright with blooms
As nature decorates her rooms
With buds and blossoms fresh and new;
Greening leaves show every hue.
Skies are azure, sunny, clear;
Rains come scattered, air wafts pure.
Days are warm, not too hot yet,
Brisk at times yet still well met.
Nights are temperate into dawn
When misty fog gives way to sun.
This is the grandest time of year;
With winter past we're happy here!

**Falling Apple Blossoms**

When apple blossoms fill the air,
Fluttering down everywhere
In a blanket of profusion,
Scattering in light confusion,
To make a bed of pink and white,
Delicate, a spring delight,
Like confetti spread around,
Sprinkling the greening ground,
We stop to gaze and contemplate
Such beauty and luxuriate
In this gift brought on by spring
Only briefly lingering,
Magic for a little while:
Bright petals falling bring a smile.

**Magnolias in the Daylight**

Magnolias in the daylight,
What a lovely sight,
Bringing us delight
With their flowers white,
While offering a view
In the spring that's new,
Bringing fragrance to
Our senses as they do,
Which by any measure
Gives our senses pleasure
To enjoy at leisure
And memories to treasure
When sweet we smell the breeze
Wafting through these trees.

## Lilies of the Valley

Lilies of the Valley
Opening today,
Delicate and tiny
In their modest way,
Ever unassuming,
Growing near the ground,
Perfect white and blooming,
Spreading all around,
Make a garden border,
Accents with a curve
Giving form and order
As they gently serve
For the eye a pleasure,
Pleasing beyond measure.

## When Zephyrs Whoosh and Blow

When zephyrs whoosh and blow
Upon the earth below,
On days like this we go
Outdoors to and fro
To feel the waves of wind
Till darkening clouds move in,
And soon the rains begin
With thunderous lightning din.
Then afterwards there's peace
As clouds the sun release,
And winds relax and cease,
North, south, west and east.
What a pleasant day
To stay outside and play!

## An Evening Still and Fair

Moon in repose is pale tonight—
Veiled by clouds it is not bright—
Yet here the evening's still and fair
With lilacs bringing scented air.
How mellow dusk is, and one knows
The flowers, too, seem in repose
With dainty leaves the shape of hearts
And many tiny flower parts
On each stem of purple hue
Opened lately fresh and new,
Standing lovely there to see,
Fragrant in their majesty
All around our garden seat
Inside a pergola—how sweet!

## The Midnight Moon

The midnight moon glides slowly
Across the cloudy sky,
Descending, moving lowly,
Not seemingly to fly.
It shows no hint of hurry,
No harsh anxiety,
And has no need to worry
About where it must be.
It has been here before,
A pattern ages set,
And will be many more,
A way it won't forget,
Just follows gravity
That rules infallibly.

# II. Garden Time

## A Garden of Verses

Through my poems come visit me.
Our house is near a maple tree.
Imagine there are gardens 'round!
Hear the birds which so abound—
Treat your ears to lovely sound.

Close by our house a river runs
And widens large, a lake becomes
Where waterfowl can congregate,
Feed themselves, thrive, and mate
Till autumn when these birds migrate.

On the back deck feel sweet peace;
Relax, unwind, let stress release.
Bring imagination and a happy mood,
Feast on the view.  Here it's understood
In the mind's eye life can be good.

## Morning in the Garden

Welcome morning, rising sun
Signaling that day's begun—
Brilliant in its bright display—
Chasing shadows far away,
Drying off the early dew,
Opening daylilies new,
And lacy lilacs in the hedge
Near our waking garden beds.
Bees fly in from busy hives;
Nectar animates their lives
And they know right where to go
Helped by ultraviolet glow
As light brings visions of rebirth
Revealing flowers on the earth.

## Garden Glory

Our garden is a glory
To plant and then attend,
An agriculture story
On which we can depend,
A pleasure where we grow
Both vegetables and flowers,
A joy we've come to know
And cultivate for hours,
A splendid sight to see
In every tidy row,
A happy ground where we
Find we often go,
And when we weed it right,
A seasonal delight.

## From Seed to Harvest

We love to plant our garden,
Scratch rows with a hoe,
Drop our hopeful seeds in
The earth and watch them grow,

See them begin their sprouting
Up above the ground,
Lifting stems and sending
Roots to grow deep down

Daily getting stronger,
Basking in the sun,
Opening up flowers
Starting to become

Juicy watermelons,
Carrots, peas, and beans,
Lettuce, cauliflower,
Chard, and other greens,

Broccoli and cucumbers,
Squash, eggplants, and corn,
In ever growing numbers
Taking sun each morn

To harvest in the fall,
With pears and apples, too.
Some we'll can for winter;
That's just what we do,

Fresh to eat, nutritious,
Scrumptious plants to taste,
Garden food delicious
To feed each happy face.

## Delicious Discovery

A strawberry is a vegetable;
A tomato is a fruit.
Each one as a whole
Is guaranteed to suit
A person who likes food
Of the yummy sort.
Both of them are good
We're happy to report.
They do assuage our hunger,
And please our palate quick—
Both of them among our
Favorites to pick.

## Ripe Strawberries

I saw a strawberry red and sweet,
Ripe and ready, good to eat,
Picked it, then pulled off its stem,
Did the same for another ten,
Washed them, filled a crystal bowl,
Poured on milk and ate them whole,
So delicious, satisfying,
Quickly, hardly realizing
Treats like these could be so good,
And only later understood
Better would have been to savor
To the utmost their fine flavor.
Had I taken twice the time,
They might have tasted *more* divine.

## Our Plastic Garden Owl

We have a plastic owl
That wears a fearsome scowl.
Although it eats no prey,
It keeps some pests away
From our garden plot,
Which really helps a lot.
As far as we're aware
Most creatures it won't scare;
Birds sit upon its head
After they have fed.
And yet the few it will,
Gives us quite a thrill,
To think with all its quirks
This plastic bird still works!

## Garden Instructions

Please do not walk or ambulate,
Peregrinate or perambulate,
Bustle, bolt, careen, or climb,
Traipse or trudge, make double-time,
Dash or dart, galumph or hop,
Hustle, shuffle, pause or stop,
Promenade or plod or prance,
Sprint or tiptoe, stomp or dance,
Jaunt or lumber, jump or shamble,
Meander, mosey, march, or amble,
Jog or skip, sidle, slink,
Stride or stroll up past the brink,
Or have to say, "I beg your pardon."
Please, do not trample through our garden.

## Weeding Time

In our garden I will go
Armed and ready with my hoe
Where a million weeds now grow
Above the dirt, also below.

And yes, I know, without a doubt,
It's difficult to dig them out.
Even if I am persistent,
Weeds are equally resistant.

I may spray and pull and rake,
Mow and swear and castigate.
Words matter not, nor plotted deeds,
For in the end there'll be more weeds,

Weeds of every kind and sort
Waiting as if to retort,
"Silly man, growth is our sport
No matter to what you resort.

"We are here, intend to stay
Hunkered down night and day,
And we'd like to let you know
We just laugh when you hoe, hoe!"

## The Hoe, My Woe

Gardener, be wary where you go,
Especially when you're near a hoe.
You call it friend, well, maybe so,
But watch your step lest hoe prove foe.

The one I stepped on gave a blow
To my head; that's how I know
That a noggin can be tender
With a bump from this offender.

It hit me hard, impressively,
And just between us, you and me,
I called it a little blankety, blank,
But only had myself to thank.

So watch the hoe you have around,
Don't leave it lying on the ground.
The truth is it can give a whack—
You step on it, it gets you back.

## Rompin' Rabbits

Rompin', hoppin', and be-boppin',
That's what hungry rabbits do
Through our garden; always happens,
Scores of rascals rampage through.

Come to nibble, they're relentless;
All our veggies they pursue.
Without fences we're defenseless
From the damage rabbits do.

May as well just hang a sign out:
"Welcome, bunnies, to the feast!
Fill your bellies, run about;
Our efforts to stop you have ceased."

Rabbits do not read, however,
Though they're clever—that's for sure—
Chomping goodies, best and better,
Any foods that they prefer.

If we had a dog to stop them
Or a pet cat that might do,
But they'd have to be around when
Rabbits choose to come and chew.

Rompin', hoppin', and be-boppin',
Rabbits visit more and more.
So, of course, we've started shoppin'
At our local grocery store.

## Bunny Defense

A tussle with bunnies
Was waged here every day.
'Cause bunnies wanted veggies;
"Too bad!" is what we'd say.

They're seriously hungry,
Determined, and they're smart.
If they could have their way
They'd fill a grocery cart.

From lettuce by the head,
And carrots by the bunch,
It hardly needs be said
They'd love to take a munch

For lunch or brunch, whenever,
To feast till full, and when
They'd won at this endeavor,
They'd do it all again.

We'd chase them; we'd call, "Scat!"
We'd shout out, "Bunnies, scram!"
But they would eat till fat
Because that was their plan.

But now we have a fence
That's solidly in place,
We're well protected, hence,
No bunnies need we chase.

The veggies are all ours,
Ours and ours alone.
Let bunnies use their powers
To go and grow their own!

## My Groundhog

The groundhog underneath my shed
Makes its home with dirt its bed,
Lives there without paying rent,
Seems to like it, quite content,

Lurks around my yard and eats
Flowers and veggies—thinks they're treats,
Digs new tunnels, that's its game.
Its underground home is its claim to fame.

I see it and occasionally
Catch it looking back at me.
What's it thinking? I don't know.
Likely that it'd wish I'd go.

What am I with it to do,
Frown and mope or say, "Hey, shoo?"
Shoo, indeed! It plans to stay
And I can't make it go away,

Not while I am more than kind,
Though I've more than half a mind
To smoke it out, end its buffet,
Immediately and then to say:

"Get thee gone, thou critter furry!
Run, vamoose, and in a hurry.
Find another place to eat,
Not from my garden, I repeat.

Besides, my shed is not for rent,
Not to a mammal or rodent.
Take a hint from this, my poem,
And find yourself another home!"

## Windy Day

The wind last night got in its licks,
Downed rotten branches and weak sticks,
Scattered them on sodden ground
Hither, thither, all around;
Amazing what the wind can do
With limbs to break. It blew and threw
Twigs beneath the maple tree,
Left lawn in chaos. It's up to me
To clean the mess and cart away
Brittle branchlets where they lay
That wind had pruned, a startling sight
For me to find by morning's light.
It took two hours till I was done
Addressing nature's night of fun.

------

Note: Please be careful not to go under trees on windy days and afterwards watch out for caught branches in trees ready to fall.

## Yard Work

I spent an hour on my yard
This morning; it was hot and hard
Clearing leaves and lots of sticks,
Watching out for bees and ticks.
It is a task I often do—
Daily almost I pursue—
Until my yard looks clean and neat,
The most attractive on my street
For its size, which is to say,
A whole lot better than okay.
I've added flowers for more color,
Showy annuals like none other,
With my stately oak for shade
Paying dividends by age,
Adding to my river view.
It's work like this I love to do.

P.S. I'll add, it's never through!

## Rainy Morning

Morning comes on rainy, slow;
Fast the grass is going to grow.
Set to flourish, grass depends
On rain and sun, which each extends
By grace of springtime in this clime,
Raindrops coming right in time.
Then roots are nourished warm and wet
With the liquid gold they get.
Up will come green sprouts anew
Filling spaces as they do,
The grass awaiting each sun ray
Responding to the lengthening day.

## Storm Brings Green

A gentle breeze begins the day
And heralds storm to come.
Clouds grow gray and soon convey
A mood that's heavy, glum.

Neighbors beat a house retreat
As rain brings on a chill;
Lawns get soggy down the street
And bird baths start to fill.

Now the wind with fury lashes
Branches like a whip,
Rattling shutters, and the sashes
Shake as though they'll rip.

Finally, the storm blows past;
The sun at last is seen
Glowing on the sodden grass,
Once dormant, now turned green.

Then in the air a bright-hued bow
Arcs across the sky,
Bringing hope to earth below
When the storm's passed by.

# III. When Mowing Harkens

## Dew, Adieu

Dew has gathered on the grass;
Every blade is wet,
Each drop like a jewel that has
Been polished, placed, and set.
The sun will soon be at its station
Warming up our lawn,
Working at evaporation
Until the dew is gone.
Humidity here still remains,
Though wind is on its way;
Soon it will take extra pains
To blow the dew away.
And when the drops have gone, just so,
We'll likely go outside and mow.

## Mowing At Leisure

As summer rains come and go
And make my lawn of green grass grow,
Once again it's time to mow
Back and forth, row by row.
Though a chore to some may be,
I enjoy it since I see
Progress right ahead of me,
Feeling footloose, fancy free.
It's a periodic pleasure
Hard to quantify or measure,
But for me it serves as leisure,
A cheerful task I actually treasure,
One that when it's done, complete,
Makes my yard look trim and neat.

## When Mowing Harkens

The summer comes with heat turned on
And with it rain to grow my lawn.
My leisure of the winter gone,
Mowing harkens with the dawn.
But not before the morning dew
Evaporates can I pursue
The cutting of the grass I do.
When this task is finished, through,
I am covered thick with sweat,
Dripping, soaked, completely wet,
Stinky as a man can get.
Then the challenge has been met,
Making all my turf conform
To a three-inch height. Ah, uniform!

## The Visitor

A visitor I met today
Passing through my lawn;
I barely got the briefest glance
Of this phenomenon.

A garter snake it was for sure;
No gender could I see,
But I can say this, as for fear:
It engendered none in me.

I did not chase it as it fled
Since I was big, it small,
But only wished to say "Hello,"
And watch it move, that's all.

It slithered rapidly from sight
With clever locomotion;
Its zigzags on the grass so light
Caused not the least commotion.

In just an instant it moved on
Too fast to interfere.
It came, it went, and then was gone;
That's how snakes disappear.

## Trim Grass

My grass has spread in all directions
Without a shred of my intentions.
Bravely, some has faced the blade,
With every pass my lawnmower's made.
Most goes flying everywhere,
Cut to the quick; I do not care
As I cross my yard and cut
Fescue and I know not what,
Weeds, perhaps, that grow or grew
On my land, more than a few.
I do my cutting at an hour
When it's cool with mower power,
Which is what I always do
To make my grass look trim and new.

## Grass Too Long

My grassy lawn has grown too long.
Now what am I to do?
This happened fast while I was gone;
Rain came and so it grew.

Because this did not happen slow
Now it is too high to mow,
And all it wants to do is grow.
What to do? I hardly know.

I had a thought how to begin;
I'd call a local service in.
They asked me warily on the phone,
"How long has it been

Since the last time it was cut?"
I said, "Eight weeks." And they said, "What!
How many inches is it now?"
"Ten," I answered. They said, "Wow!

"That's far more than we allow.
Go hire some goats or rent a cow!"

## Kicking Grass

I came, I mowed, and kicked some grass;
My turf was getting long.
I had to, for you see, alas,
It grew too thick and strong.

For if I do not cut my grass,
The grass will grow unruly,
Get uppity and even sass;
It will, I tell you truly.

I cannot let the grass just be.
One minute it seems short,
But add rain and humidity
And soon it will resort

To rising up unlike it was
To occupy a field.
I've seen it done with little pause
Intending not to yield.

I cut it down, I fertilize,
And then before I know it,
My grass grows back before my eyes,
Impossible to slow it.

Inch by inch it works and hard;
I watch it to discern
How it grows up yard by yard
Plotting its return.

Then I have to mow once more,
Clip and snip and trim.
There is no choice, it is a chore
Not optional, no whim

That can be simply brushed aside;
My grass must be addressed.
I cannot stop, I cannot hide;
Perhaps delay at best

Is all that I can do, not long,
Or soon it's out of hand,
Past tall and lush, past carpet plush,
Till I must take a stand,

Get up and go and kick some grass,
Mow and mow some more,
Over and over, pass after pass,
Until my arms grow sore.

There is no rest; I do my best
Lest neighbors say, "Hey you!
You've missed a spot, we guess you've got
A little left to do."

I nod and smile and chat, and then
I wipe away my sweat,
Agreeing, yes, then start again;
No point to get upset,

'Cause grass is grass and grass just grows,
And summer grass grows faster.
I own it: better own my woes.
The grass is my taskmaster!

―――――――
With a nod to Louis Untermeyer's "Long Feud."

## A Lawn Going to Weeds

When spring has come, winter gone,
I choose to contemplate my lawn
Before the grass has grown too long,

And there, just starting up, will come
Weeds, ten thousand, not just some,
Demanding space beneath the sun.

What am I to do with them,
Considering that weeds have been
First to claim their places when

The welcome warming rays of sun
Have invited them to come?
And did they ever on the run!

Some might say to spray those critters,
But feed and weed gives me the jitters,
Especially when I hear twitters

From the birds that fly around
Healthy with a happy sound,
Often eating on the ground.

So I am stumped. What to do?
It's not as if the problem's new,
Only this year more weeds grew.

In my mind I must debate here,
Do I yield to Mother Nature,
Or address the problem later?

Should I simply let weeds grow
And ruin my grass? I don't know,
Or just leave them, only mow?

Really, I don't have a clue,
No idea what to do.
Help me reader, what would you?

# IV. Letter To a Dandelion

## Dandelions Like Stars

Much like a field of glowing stars,
Our yard this summer has become
Graced by dandelions spread sparse,
Each one like a little sun,
Golden yellow in its bloom,
Waiting till it goes to seed,
Hoping for sufficient room
As may meet its growing need.
Soon the wind will have a say,
All their tiny seeds to scatter,
Blowing near and far each day,
To new places they can gather
Where they soon will multiply
Again like stars that fill the sky.

## Dandelions Like Grass

The grass must know
When spring has come
That soon the sun
Will help it grow,
And dandelions will try invade—
Pernicious as they come—
Though homeowners have likely paid
A service to treat some.
Alas, these wanton weeds get through
By methods known for stealth
No matter what folks try to do
To keep their turf in health.
It makes an owner dream of laws
Weeds might respect or give them pause.

## Letter to a Dandelion

Dear Dandelion,

What shall we do
To spare our lawn the likes of you,
To keep your yellow blooms and seed
From blowing, spreading like a weed?

We try to find you early, spray
Before you spring up every May.
We know you think you're lovely, fair,
And want to pop up everywhere

When weather warm gets you excited,
But know this: you are not invited
Except to vanish (please, and fast),
Not occupy our pretty grass.

We would so much appreciate
If you would move, evacuate.
Is that too much to ask of you,
To say to us, "Just passing through?"

To never even plan to stop
Nor your fluffy seeds to drop?

With due respect, if not affection,

The Weed Department of Inspection

# The Dandelion's Reply

To: The Weed Department of Inspection

Be advised I've read your letter,
And frankly, you don't get it yet, or
It stems from ignorance, you see,
And lack of understanding me.

Just to begin, I'm not a weed!
I'm more than that. My message heed:
I am a bona fide flower with roots in the ground,
No need to spread those rumors around.

Your letter brings me consternation,
Disparaging my true vocation,
Which, as you know, is propagation,
Making seeds and their transportation.

That is why your characterization
Of me as a weed without reservation
Is mistaken, false, untrue,
And so let me enlighten you.

The shape of my leaves is in my name—
It's from the French—since they look the same
As a *dent de lion*, meaning lion's tooth,
Along the edges, and that's the truth.

My family and I came from the East
Where for centuries we lived in peace,
Expanded our range into China
Prized for our flowers, none found fina.

And further, we went on to Japan
Not easily done, but by planters' plan,
And we prospered there as well,
As our history does tell.

My kind has been a daring rover
With 200 types and, moreover,
We're famous for our variety,
Recognized by the National Dandelion Society.

Long cultivated, we've paid our dues,
And come embellished in many hues,
Not just the yellow familiar to you,
But white, orange, black, and copper, too,

Which apparently you did not know.
Both tall and short are ways we grow,
Found in gardens back in the day.
What an important part we play

In providing pollen to the honeybee,
And mind you, this we do for free!
Without us, we just do not know
Where the honeybee would go.

Remember, too, from ancient times
Our flowers have made delicious wines
That we have given to the cause
Of liquid pleasure. Please, applause!

For bouquets and tonics, coffee, too,
Rubber from our sap, and roots for stew,
And as an herb to protect your health
With vitamin C and iron, better than wealth,

While your fellow human beings
Enjoy our leaves as salad greens.
In all these ways we're more than good
For Earth, for you, for bees, and should

Be treated with kindness and respect,
Not purged. Is this too much to expect?
Our nature is noble, not to despise.
So in conclusion, to summarize,

I'm who I am, proud to be here.
Do you understand? Is this clear?
Live and let live and we'll get along
To share our planet where we belong.

Hoping for a better relationship,
For working this out, here's a little tip:
There's still a place for me out of doors!
I am most humbly and truly yours,

*Dan D. Dandelion*

----------------------
Caveat: The author is referring to cultivated dandelions grown under horticultural conditions from food-quality sources for herbal use in small quantities. Please do not pick or consume any wild dandelion parts from neighborhood lawns or from the curbside, which may be contaminated with lawn chemicals, car exhaust, animal waste, or otherwise be unsafe.

## Apology Letter to a Dandelion

Dear Dandelion,

What can we say
About our letter of the other day
And your dismay we've libeled you?
We apologize—it's the least we can do.

We've had a change of heart, you see;
Please accept our apology.
We realize now we've done you wrong,
And so we're singing a different song,

Especially for calling you just a weed.
It wasn't fair, tactless indeed.
You actually are an historical herb
With a pedigree that is superb.

But for plants of your stature
The lawn's no place to grow.
It's not that safe, that's for sure,
Since we frequently mow.

We hope you don't mind
And please beg our pardon
If we keep dandelions
Confined to our garden.

In this way we can advocate
For your herbal protection.

Sincerely, and your cooperation we await,

The Weed Department of Inspection

## Summer Weeds

Today I went and cut my grass.
It's grown a lot; it really has,
Row by row, pass by pass,
Chop, chop, chop, I mowed a path.

And after that I trimmed another
Exposing weeds hid undercover,
Dandelions and such as these
Which, of course, did not me please.

You know the ones—they just show up.
I wish they'd stop. I've had enough!
Yet they return persistently,
Expecting me to let them be.

They pop up from their tiny seeds,
To thrive and grow with little leaves,
Which leaves a quandary, what to do?
Spray or pull? I wish I knew.

Why won't they stop, give up the fight?
Why do they stick around—for spite?
Each spring I try to make them go,
But still they show up, grow and grow,

And will, no doubt, till I'm long gone,
Still re-invade our hapless lawn.
And so I say to friends, don't miss
The fact your lawn could come to this,

In truth most likely soon, not later,
Unwanted plants, each new invader,
Can strike your lawn, and hence I mention
To weeds we'd best pay close attention,

Or rest assured, they will take over,
And I'm not speaking just of clover,
But spurweed, bindweed, and by golly
Cudweed, trefoil, creeping Charlie,

Purslane, mint—herbs for the garden
Unwanted in the lawn or yard—and
Henbit, chickweed, pennywort, plaintain—
Foraged plants not for grass plantin'.

Then there's pusley, pesky thistle,
Knotweed, filaree—all of these will
Fill our days with worry, sorrow—
Not to mention ragweed, yarrow,

Wild onion, too, and dread bellflower.
Crabgrass and quackgrass to make us holler,
And broadleaf weeds—there are so many
We do not want or need, not any.

To these we say, "You weeds, be gone!
We just want you off our lawn!"
When they're about we root them out,
Although no doubt they'll still resprout.

Our best defense is longer grass,
To mow less often for this has
(Along with mulch) held some weeds back
From their usual plan of attack.

But this, alas, goes just so far;
We turn our backs and there they are
Again, determined, bound to try
Spread about both low and high,

Far and wide, hither and yon.
They're just that clever, rarely gone.
They'll fight our fescue, roam our lawn
Like Caesar crossing the Rubicon!

## Confronting Creeping Charlie

Lo, 'tis the season of sweet spring
When light rains caress our lawn,
And we look forward to its greening
With winter finally gone.

Rich as velvet our grass stands
Thick and lush, our joy, our prize.
All its care rests in our hands,
So we tend and fertilize.

How our grass thrives with careful mowing,
Emerald glowing in the sun,
Like a carpet ever growing,
It impresses everyone.

With loving care meticulous,
We are watchful, vigilant,
Meeting all threats numerous
To keep our lawn luxuriant.

Yet in spite of all our efforts,
Our devotion and great care,
Irrespective of our labors,
And the toils that we must bear,

There is one vandal, green invader,
Interloping every day.
No matter our resolve, this raider
Conspires to drop by and to stay.

We mean *you*, Creeping Charlie,
Spreading over our fine lawn;
Though we pull you almost daily,
Still we cannot get thee gone.

How you grow, advance, and prosper
And degrade our lovely grass!
You're no fescue, you imposter;
You are merely crude and crass.

Though we admit you do look pretty,
Violet-flowered in the spring,
You're the scourge of town and city:
You'd like to cover everything.

You're as bad, almost, as kudzu,
Dreadful as the dandelion.*
Sneaky, twisty, stealthy, too,
Like a snake you're serpentine.

When you evade our protections,
We'll still fight you every day,
You with all your fine connections,
That indicate you plan to stay.

And though you put us in a sweat,
In defense, we say, "En garde!"
We shall vanquish you, thou varlet.
Do you hear us? Off our yard!

----------------
* Oh, no! I'm going to get another
letter from the dandelions!

## Weeds We Inherit

The weeds that we inherit
Are hiding underground.
We may not quite admit it,
But that is where they're found
Waiting for a chance
To spring up and to grow,
Thrive as they advance
Quickly, seldom slow,
Leafing out for sun,
Soaking up the rain.
When all's said and done,
Over and over again
They still spread everywhere,
Here and all about
With more seeds to spare
Until we root them out!

## Buckthorn Trees

In a corner of our yard
Buckthorn plants appeared one day,
Though we have worked extra hard
To keep invasive weeds at bay.

Buckthorn trees have living will;
They rarely ever die.
In any bare patch they can fill
They live on, or they try.

Their roots are strong and so they keep
On clinging, never knowing
That we work for their defeat;
They take the long view growing.

Disposal means to dig their roots
Out till none remain,
Nothing there to let new shoots
Re-grow and start again.

Even then one must take care
To remove every strand;
With just a wisp they can repair
Themselves and make a stand.

This isn't a conspiracy
The way they grow persistently;
It's simply that tenacity
Is in the nature of this tree.

## Crabgrass

All this summer, off and on,
I have sat upon my lawn
Pulling crabgrass by its roots,
And so with time my lawn now looks

Better; still the fight's not over
With other weeds, including clover,
Which keep on coming back, I see,
Constantly, persistently.

Often, when I've found it urgent,
I've put down a pre-emergent,
And while this has helped a little
Around the edge and in the middle

For established crabgrass tough
This is simply not enough,
Though I persist and don't despair,
Working at it here and there.

Yet I know when I shall die,
Turn to dust in the sweet by and by,
That the crabgrass will be back
With a vengeance and a laugh!

# V. Flights of Summer

## Sunrise

The sunrise born this morning
Brings blended colors bright,
A tapestry adorning
A sky of golden light
No painter could devise
Reflected on the lake—
Its brilliance a surprise—
A wonder of daybreak.
Vivid colors imbued
With richness dust has made,
 Create a dazzling interlude
To watch until they fade,
Washed out by rising light
With passing of the night.

## Morning

Traces of the night
Were fading from our sight,
The morning coming on
With wonders of the dawn.
Gone were animals
That forage after dark.
Then we heard bird calls
As if announcing, "Hark!
A new day has begun;
It's time to be about.
Wake up, everyone!
The sun is coming out
Warmly on its way.
Celebrate today!"

## Robin's Reveille

Like reveille a robin sings
To me each early morn.
When I'm sound asleep he brings
His voice to me inform:
"It's time to get up, lazybones.
You're dozing late—what for?"
This in his most insistent tones
When I would rather snore.
"I'm tired," I groan. "Please let me take
A few more winks, you know?"
By then, of course, I'm wide awake
So I rise, get up, and go.

## Birds of Summer

When birds of summer sing, we hear
Their happiness and know they're near
Having fun in daring flight,
Using wings with feathers bright,
The males especially this way
Have colors bold in bright array
From early May well into fall
When hints of winter start to call.
Yet many then won't seem to care.
Instead they glory in the air,
With wings so agile, quick and strong,
They'll just keep singing, chirping on
In imitation of their friends,
A joy until the season ends.

## Our Bird Feeders

In the morning birds will come
To our feeders, one by one,
Orioles and hummers, too,
And other birds, often new,
Such a pleasure ours to see
Here for breakfast served for free
Time and time and time again,
Each one sure to entertain
As we watch them, such a pleasure,
Filling up at their leisure,
Sometimes feeding two by two,
Side by side as they do,
Knowing now they can rely
On a feast when they fly by.

## Birdie at Our Feeder

Hello, birdie, at our feeder;
It's your lucky day to be here.
And it's clear, happily,
You love to drink our sugar tea
As we watch while this occurs
Using our binoculars
Focused on you with intent,
To see you drink; it's evident
What we offer here is sweet,
Just for you, a special treat
As you belly to the bar—
Better than some bugs by far—
And you seem grateful, friend, to be
Flying in to drink for free!

## The Baltimore Oriole

The oriole from Baltimore,
Black and golden in decor,
Will razzle-dazzle when you've heard
The singing of this brilliant bird.
If you would have them at your feeder,
Slice an orange and they will be there
To enjoy this lovely treat
Delectable and sweet to eat.
You need to watch if you would see
An oriole there frequently.
Be very patient when you try it,
Always careful to stay quiet,
And when you do, you will adore
This bird that's named for Baltimore.

## Our Baltimore Orioles

We can scarcely express the degree of delight
We feel at our living room window to sight
Baltimore orioles as they appear
To drink at our feeders for hummingbirds here.
As we sit watching them coming to feed
On sweet sugar water as is their need.
This is the first year we are aware
Of having not one, but two, a pair!
Each one comes flying in for its fill
Striving to drink all it can with its bill
While we rejoice that both of them got here
To indulge their great thirst with our sugar water,
Sharing it daily with many a hummer
Also in residence here for the summer.

## The Joy of Hummingbirds

Bright hummingbirds go flit, flit, flit,
Then they slowly hover
At our feeder's perch a bit—
These birds are like no other!
Not only forward can they fly
But backwards just as well;
They hardly even seem to try
As far as we can tell.
Acrobats they are for sure
While zipping through the air;
So quick they are that as it were
We hardly know they're there,
But often watch them come at dawn
To drink—then in a wink they're gone.

## A Blue Jay's Intentions

A blue jay landed on a limb
As we sat near watching him,
Guessing what his thoughts might be
While he perched there in the tree.
Was he contemplating lunch,
As we surmised, though just a hunch,
Or had he landed for a rest
In his feathers smartly dressed?
Was he looking for a flock
Of fellow jays with whom to talk
To decide if he should stay
Here for winter or fly away?
What it was he planned to do
Before he flew we never knew.

## Dawn Visit

Today at dawn, guess what came
And crossed my lawn, a whooping crane!
Gray and graceful, slim and tall,
Silently it made its call,
Walked as if it were unsure
Where it was going, as it were;
Stopped and stood in feathered grace
So briefly we were face-to-face.
I watched, enthralled, to see it pass
And wander on across the grass.
Unreal it seemed in the extreme
Like some strange moment in a dream
When I alone was privileged there
To glimpse this famous bird, so rare.

## One Summer Day

When summer came, to our surprise
One day it brought bright butterflies.
Dozens of them filled the air
Fluttering near everywhere.
How, we wondered, could this be?
They'd all appeared so suddenly
In our garden by the lake.
What of this were we to make?
Magic, maybe, born of bliss,
More than metamorphosis;
So it seemed this special day
With nature's beauty on display,
Way above mere expectation,
A wonder for our exaltation.

## Butterfly Wings

Opening its royal wings
The monarch butterfly
Is a wonder when it flings
Its body through the sky,
Daring, delicate and small,
Beautiful and bright,
Confident it will not fall
In its fearless flight.
Searching for a flower,
It carefully will land
With grace and awesome power
When it stops to stand
For a moment not to waste
On a blossom sweet to taste.

## Majestic Monarch

Butterfly, butterfly, don't flit away.
True, you are busy, but stay today, stay.
The garden we planted has milkweed you need
To lay your small eggs where your offspring can feed.
Flutter here, stay about, rest another day;
Later on you'll journey south, happy on your way.
Butterfly, butterfly, first pupa, then chrysalis,
Nature transforms you by metamorphosis.
You float with wings so bright, like a fairy sprite,
Fluttering in flight, perfect, such delight!
Monarch, royal butterfly, with wings of regal glory
That nature lifts on high—remarkable your story!
Butterfly, butterfly, bright orange and free,
So lovely, you rule in light majesty.

## The Dainty Moth

The moth's regalia,
Delicate to see,
Has fine feathered feelers
Fragile as can be.
Almost too light to weigh,
Slighter than we know,
In flight each summer day,
We watch it come and go:
Flutters to a leaf,
Makes the briefest stay,
Gaining short relief
To rest, then flies away.

## To a Tree

Rise up tree branches
With arms that touch the sky;
Limbs with leaves you've made
Hold songbirds safe on high.

Your shoulders wide arrayed
Shelter us below
Where we sit in shade
Grateful that you grow.

## Renditions of the Wren

Renditions of the wren
Add music to my day,
And this has always been
A special joy, a way
To give my life a lift,
A measure of delight.
A song that is a gift
Bestowed before its flight
Is nature's way to say,
"Have a happy day!"

# VI. Golden Days of Summer

**Morning Sun**

The sun grows vivid bringing day,
Burns the valley fog away,
Rises over ridge and rill
Chasing off the morning chill,
Till gradually its bright array
Paints pink highlights that will stay
Moments only, then move on,
Fading fast with coming dawn
That bathes the day in dazzling light—
This marvelous view a pleasing sight—
Bringing wonder after night:
Morning glory and delight.

## Crystal Rainbow Morning

The sun was shining, in it came
Past flowers bowing to its flame,
Past curtain lace and windowsill,
Beaming, bringing light to spill,
Flooding house with warming wave
Flinging the bright cheer it gave
Through crystal prisms as it rose,
Speckling walls with small rainbows,
Flecks of magic here and there
At random scattered through the air.
This is how the day began
Spontaneous, without a plan,
Hours unfolding after night
With dappled colors of delight.

**Morning Glory Story**

The morning glory's careful climb
Is helped by rain and sun and time
As with hope its tendrils try
To stretch and cling and rise up high
Upon our fence,
And onward hence,
All its strength it will apply
To reach upward to the sky.
Its spiral blossoms as they grow
Are beautiful in sunlight's glow
Each morning at its special hour
Of blooming glory: flower power!

## Summer Iris

Summer Iris
Lithe and slender
In my eyes
Green engender
Beauty rising
To the fore
From their verdant
Garden floor.
Vibrant as they
Strive to climb
Ever taller,
These I find
Exquisite
In their majesty—
Nature's art
Enthralling me.

## Bushes Blocking Windows

House bushes keep on growing,
Our windows soon to hide
Until there's no way knowing
Inside what's hid outside.
Our house feels isolated
From any open view;
The bushes have negated
The sight that once we knew.
The door is our salvation;
It lets us go outside
To see with contemplation
What now our bushes hide:
A lovely stretch of lawn
We'd see were bushes gone.

## The Thrush

From deep within the underbrush
Sings a sweet soprano thrush.
Why he's happy no one knows,
Yet it is clear he's one of those
Who is a cheerful little bird,
One you often may have heard
Even if you couldn't see
Him making lovely melody,
Brightening the very air,
Joyful, like he has no care,
Raising up his song on high,
Pleasing any passerby
Who might pause to hear his sound,
Music sung to all around.

## Silver Maple Seeds

Windmills by the thousands
Are falling from our tree,
Fluttering and spinning
To the ground we see.
Even though the odds
For doing so are low,
They're hoping for the chance
To land where they may grow.

## The Tree Next Door

Our neighbor's tree next door had stood
So long it once was in a wood,
But now alone its massive size
Encroached the house it stood beside.
New owners said it must come down,
Next to their house just north of town,
And so two people came with saws
To cut it—not against the laws.
And part by part chainsaw went at it,
Motor straining, while from our attic
I watched them drop its branching height,
Saw it fall—a dreadful sight—
Until its trunk had hit the mud,
Teetered, toppled with a thud!

## Watching Squirrels

We like to watch squirrels every day
When to our yard they come to play,
Running hither, hopping there,
Relaxed it seems without a care,
Starting early every morn,
Hunting for each ripe acorn
They had hidden in the fall,
A splendid feast as they recall.
Who needs a mall or grocery store
When squirrels have plenty, even more
Than many other creatures do,
Which they dig up and pursue
Holding acorns in their claws,
Feasting almost without pause.

## Squirrel Story

A squirrel crept down his maple tree
And leapt along. He did not see
Me watching him above and still
Standing at my windowsill.

I studied him while looking down
To where he scampered on the ground
Till presently he climbed the stair
Beside my house right up to where

A water dish on my deck rail
Was empty, dry, and so turned tail
About to leave decidedly
When suddenly he noticed me.

I had to laugh at his surprise—
The way he gazed into my eyes—
Then quick surmised I meant no harm,
Which seemed to quell his first alarm.

He turned, ran back, then up his tree
Where safety was a certainty.
Since then in mind I oft review
His shock when face-to-face, we two,

The way we were just standing there,
The squirrel and I, stare by stair.

## Dragonfly Engineering

A dragonfly was flying by
Our house's deck built up high
Overlooking our backyard and
Our little flower garden

That has a splendid oak tree view
(But back to the dragonfly for you).
This creature, though, had not two wings,
But two pair, most amazing things,

That work in concert, four together,
Precisely engineered—how clever.
And so this dragonfly I saw
Could hover in the air and yaw

Side to side, then quickly turn
As I observed with much to learn.
To look at it was more than pleasant,
Like a stick with eyes, all iridescent,

And though its weight is clearly light
For what it does, its wings have might
That help it fly fast as a wink,
Remarkable—don't you think?

And so next time a dragonfly
Near my deck should happen by,
I shall note with special care
How well it navigates the air.

## Chipmunks

Consider chipmunks, how wise their goals,
Who build their homes with many holes.
This is prudent, brilliant, even,
Preparing the ground for emergency leavin'.

If one hole is closed or becomes damaged,
These smart little critters have actually managed
To prepare another passage most cleverly,
Ready to use in an emergency.

They've thought things through, gone full bore,
Know what to do. They've dug, what's more,
Deserve real credit for foresight sound.
Do they get praised for engineering underground?

Likely never, or if so, whence?
But their insurance plan makes a "hole" lot of sense.
We admire their skill, but beg their pardon:
Prefer they not dig in our yard or garden!

## Verdant Moss

It gives me pause--I'm at a loss--
To see how steadily soft moss
Spreads across my patio
Every season, though it's slow.
It covers up the rotted stump
Of a tree long-gone now sunk
In the ground with emerald skin.
Moss has gradually moseyed in,
Invading crevices around
In scattered patches on the ground,
And, as far as I'm aware,
It travels on by wind and air.
It's verdant beauty at my feet,
Richly green, yet so petite,
Makes me ponder how it's there,
So patient, spreading everywhere.

## A Tree and Me

Today is windy and a tree
Waves its branches down at me
Almost like it knows I'm here
Admiring it this time of year
In its grandeur, strong and tall,
Silent, though it seems to call
For a moment of connection,
Tree to me, an introspection
That we're happy and we care,
Living, having time to spare,
And we're thriving, ever growing,
Sensing this and clearly knowing
Though we're different, we're aware
This windy day is ours to share.

## Sun Day

The blazing sun is shining high
In the sky, the morning dry.
The grass grown coarse, absent green,
Is standing dormant, stiff and mean.

Brittle strands like shards of glass
Are painful almost, verdance passed,
With not a hint of wind in air
Or much moisture anywhere,

Nor a prayer of any soon.
Relief from baking afternoon
Sun is sought, whose light so bright
Penetrates until the night

When there might with luck accrue
Just a touch of soothing dew,
And the day might turn to peace
Bringing darkness, heat's surcease.

## Sun Setting

The sun was setting and the sky
Was fiery red and orange up high,
The remnant of a dusty day
Warm and dry, a cloud array
That lingered, though it still showed bright
Waiting for the coming night
With shadows forming on the ground,
A time of quiet, falling sound,
While beauty showed a far horizon
Of stunning hues to keep one's eyes on
As the sky showed off with flare
A final glowing distant glare
That ended gradually the day
By slowly fading, gone away.

## Storm Clouds

The sun has faded from the sky;
New clouds are forming large on high
Along a front that's moving in,
And likely rain will soon begin.
Weather folks say we're in store
For strong winds and a huge downpour.
We feel the thick and humid air;
It's hard to know how to prepare.
The thunderclouds about to burst
Will quench farm fields of all their thirst.
Chances are that roads may flood
Covering our streets with mud;
And when this squall begins to blow
There may well be a lightning show!

## Lightning Show

It's far more than a simple spark,
Lightning, that is; watch it arc
And blast the dark, then pounding thunder,
Enough to make a person wonder
What is nature doing now?
More to the point, why and how?
To allow this great disturbance,
Of atmosphere, an occurrence
Frightening across the sky
And bound to ground electrify,
Remarkable in air, this weather,
A spectacle altogether
Grander than a picture show
High in the heavens and below.

## Afternoon Storm

Ripples crawl across the lake;
Warning winds will follow
Stronger and new waves will break,
Where the water's shallow.

Soon goes fleeing every bird
While high above each cloud
Darkens; then a crack is heard—
Thunder booming loud!

Treetop branches start to sway;
Oak leaves blow and scatter.
Hail begins its ping-pong play
Bouncing with a tatter.

Then the sky gives way: it pours,
Lashing at the ground.
Close the windows! Shut the doors!
Listen to that sound!

Pounding, pounding everywhere,
Pouring rain comes down
Till a freshness fills the air
And ozone hugs the ground.

Gradually the downpour stops,
Shades of gray turn white.
Only now a few late drops
Anticipate sunlight.

Far off then to span the sky
Nature may bestow...
Look! See there, way up high
An arching bright rainbow!

## The Rainbow Road

The Rainbow Road in the sky
Curves above us, magic, high.
Its colors thrill our gazing eye
When we happen one to spy
Made by rain when light shines through,
Far too fleeting to pursue,
Like a marvelous dream come true,
A wonder to us, me and you.
A rainbow is a natural gift
Giving every heart a lift,
Usually a light surprise
When we see one in our skies
Like a bridge beyond compare
Or heaven's staircase built on air.

# VII. Day and Night on the River

## Adorning Morning

Adorning morning comes the sun
And with its rising day begun
With chirping songs of birds we hear
Bringing early hour cheer.
How fine it is to breathe the day
With floral scents, summer's bouquet;
While lilies on the lake wake up
As if to say, "We've slept enough.
It's time our petals had their due,
White in sunlight, crisp and new,"
And dazzling dragonflies alight,
Or hover motionless in flight.
We thank you, sun, for every day
With all of nature on display.

## Birds Awake

In sylvan glade
By lapping lake
Through dark and shade
Sunbeams break.

Birds awake
In dawning light
Singing day
After night.

Light of wing
Fine of feather
Hear them sing
Songs together

Soon to make
Morning flight
On their way
Loving life

Celebrating
In their way
Life's rebirth
Each new day.

## The Lolling Lily

The lolling lily rests herself
On a lake serene
Mooring near the sheltering shore
Anchored, round and green,

Waiting for the moment when
She'll show her soft white flower
Opening in morning light
Until the evening hour.

Every bloom is her delight
With yellow in the center
Looking like a patch of light
The blazing sun has lent her.

Bright and welcoming she stays
For frogs and dragonflies
That land and sun on her and laze
Under summer skies.

## Passing Swans

On the river swans serene
Glide along, seem to stream
Absent ripples, little wake,
Moving forward, undertake
Their silent journey at first light
Relaxing after evening flight.
Silently, we watch them pass,
Water surface smooth as glass,
Dipping bills beneath the surface,
Nourishment, their certain purpose,
Foraging and going slow,
Ghostly white in mist like snow,
Early in the downy dawn
Brief as phantoms, there, then gone.

## The River Wide

The river near my house flows wide,
Magnificent to see.
Across it waterfowl glide
Serene and happily.
Some days the water stays so still
No current can be seen.
Above, bright clouds move as they will;
Below the shore is green.
Mornings here I call the best.
Fog lifts beneath the sun
Making sparkles manifest,
A million if there's one.
All nature gives our eyes a show
That thrills us with the river's glow.

## River Light

The sight of sparkles on the river
Dazzles, every wave a-flicker
With a million points of light
Magical, a-glitter, bright,
Fantastical to our view
Spread across the water blue,
More than one might ever dream,
So heavenly is such a scene.
One must see it with their eyes
Just to start and realize
What is possible, how grand
Nature is, and understand
How there comes to be such art
Great enough to move the heart.

## A Clangor of Cranes

A clangor of cranes, a raucous call,
Revealed two birds, each five feet tall,
That opened wings, began to fly
Majestically into the sky,
Before the light of day had gone,
With autumn moon soon coming on.
Off they went, each gaining height
Before the sunset brought on night,
Together winging on their way,
A sight not seen here every day,
Moving high above our river,
Keeping course to who knows whither
While we wondered, standing here,
When they'd return and reappear.

## Geese Return

As night comes on,
The moon draws near,
And geese day-gone
Will reappear.

We hear them calling,
Winging wide,
When almost falling,
Down they glide

Above the river
And come to rest,
Feathers a-quiver,
Water abreast,

Where all are safe
From daylong flight,
Each flock, each wave
Home for the night.

## Evening Magic

A quiet night, no breeze at all,
No river ripples nor bird call
Are heard, yet magic flits about
For fireflies have ventured out.
Not one mosquito to detect;
Summer's come, time to reflect
How peaceful nature here can seem—
Calm, at rest, sublime, serene—
On a dreamy evening made for sleep.
Day fades to darkness, drowsy, deep,
Except our lawn shows scattered light
From lightning bugs, each a delight,
Surprising when their kin appears
With tiny blinking derrières.

## Night on the River

The hour of dusk comes calling, calling;
Sure and soon light fades away.
Apollo, sun, is leaving, leaving,
Lending clouds their red array.

Meanwhile, Luna, rising, rising,
Shows her fullness bright all night;
Stars above her, sparkling, sparkling,
Wink awake with blinking light.

Crickets start their chirping, chirping,
Almost like a symphony,
Nocturnal creatures, waking, waking,
Singing their sweet harmony.

On the river blowing, blowing,
Wind brings ripples more and more,
Water moving, waving, waving,
Gently lapping to the shore.

Night is bathed in beauty, beauty,
Graced by pine trees all around,
Slender needles whisper, whisper,
In the wind a restful sound.

Nature tells us stories, stories
Along the river on display,
Many marvels, glories, glories
As the daylight fades away.

## Captivating Crickets

Captivating crickets
In their synchronicity
Make the night a trilling concert
All around, surrounding me.

In enchanting foggy night
When the moon glows halo-bright,
Charming chirping crickets chanting
Tune my ears to their delight.

Their calling is enthralling
In a mystic mimic way,
Every insect a musician
Making magic as they play,

A great rhapsody of romance
Or menagerie of strife
In a striving for survival
In the daring dance of life.

Crickets calling in the thicket
In their harmony with kin
Sound a symphony sonorous
Over time and time again.

Play on crickets all in rhythm,
Harmonize in grass and glade,
Thrill me with your cavatina,
Sing your nocturne serenade.

## The Gibbous Moon

The gibbous moon was out tonight
Giving us its partial light,
Lovely and a welcome sight
Even though not wholly bright.
The stars were as they often are,
Twinkle-twinkling from afar
Against the night sky dark as tar,
A sparkling contrast to admire.
Spanning space for us to see
Was our Milky Way galaxy,
Detectable to some degree
Collectively and brilliantly,
All of these a splendid sight
For our eyes to view this night.

## In the Dot-to-Dot Sky

Twinkling in the dot-to-dot sky
Constellations move up high
In the nighttime, always winking,
Beyond earth satellites circling, blinking:
Ursa Major and Minor, too,
Cygnus the Swan flying through,
With Aquila and Lyra in a Triangle ... there!
Cepheus and Cassiopeia sitting on air
Near Andromeda; also Leo the Lion,
Sirius and Libra, and the hunter Orion,
Capricornus, Corona Borealis,
Hercules and Sagittarius—
These constellations, to name a few,
Are northern stars sending light to you.

# VIII. Leaves on Grass

## Inklings of Fall

It's been a good day, all in all,
With inklings of the coming fall,
A leaf dropped here, a pine cone there,
A certain crispness in the air,
The smell of leaves at twilight burning,
Squirrels working extra hard returning
Time and time again to bury
Acorns, mostly cache-and-carry.
At night, a chilly breeze comes blowing;
Grass begins to feel frost growing;
Water on the pond is calm
With hints of ice soon coming on.
It is a time of expectation,
Summer's end, fall's transformation.

## When Fall Has Come

When fall has come, suddenly
Trees transform themselves to be
Artfully, magically
Dressed in colors painterly.

Oranges, browns and reds are seen
And yellows where there once was green.
The foliage displayed for all
Reminds one of a carnival

Bright and gaudy, yet somehow
Lovely, bringing us to "wow!"
Though transient, soon to go
Giving way to cold and snow.

While still fall hues and views infuse
Our memories; we will not lose
Impressions of their brilliant glory,
Part of nature's changing story.

## Fall's Grandeur

When autumn comes I let my eyes
Enjoy the colors with surprise.
The yellows, oranges and the reds
Blanket our spent flower beds.
Tree after tree I love to see,
Their colors a bright panoply:
Maples, sumac, elms, and oaks
Wearing dazzling leafy cloaks
In the highest hues of fashion,
Put on, so it seems, with passion,
Showing off what they can do
Before their autumn show is through.
All this grandeur, nature's gift,
Gives my spirit quite a lift!

## Cruising Leaves

Leaves come cruising down,
Falling all around,
Covering the ground,
Silent, absent sound.
Such a scene as this
Brings bliss, serenity
I never wish to miss
Beneath my maple tree,
Brief in season's time,
But while it lasts, sublime.

## When Leaves Let Go

Like little birds, fall leaves let go
From branches, flit to earth below—
Flocks of them this time of year,
Almost alive it would appear—
And then lie still or mostly so
Till bursts of wind arise and blow
To scatter them by leaps and bounds
Across the lawn with rustling sounds.
It almost seems to be a game,
Some acting wildly, others tame,
Depending on each leaf profile
To catch the breeze or wait awhile
Till gradually, past skip or hop
They settle down and finally stop.

## Racing with Leaves

Autumn dawns and more leaves come
From treetops tumbling one by one.
This was not that unexpected,
But raking them I am elected,
Delegated to clear them off
While winds are blowing them aloft,
Sending them into a swirl.
Like little kites they twist and twirl.
Regardless, this work must be done—
Good exercise and sometimes fun.
So with rake I rake and rake,
Do the task without a break
Knowing tomorrow more will come.
Races with leaves are never won.

## Leaves and More Leaves

Under my silver maple tree
The yard is deep with leaves.
More keep falling steadily
Landing where they please.

Brown against my dark green grass,
Many yellow, too,
More accumulate, alas;
When will they be through?

Every time I go and rake,
More replace those gone.
Should I stop or hesitate,
They'll cover my whole lawn.

What's the use? We need a truce,
My maple tree and me,
Like I've made with several spruce
On my property.

It isn't going to happen, though;
These leaves will keep on coming,
Now and even past the snow,
With volume vast and stunning.

Come next spring, I'll rake again
As buds burst forth anew
To clear what old leaves still remain
Like I always do.

Exercise, I tell myself,
That raking leaves gives me
Is beneficial to my health,
So thank you, maple tree!

## Leaf Exercise

Fall leaves, like little fluttering birds,
Have flit from every bough.
Our trees held fast until wind stirred
Them to the ground, and now
They lie around in disarray,
So many it is hard
To bag them up or rake away
From my front and back yard.
I have no power riding mower
With collector bins behind
To drive across such piles as these,
Which leaves me in a bind.
The time it takes to rake is hours,
In fact, extends to days,
And all this work while fighting wind
That blows them random ways.
Yes, I could hire it done for sure
And save some days now lost.
Some firms would do it in an hour
Or two, but at what cost?
I'm frugal; that is just my way.
I do not wish to pay
To have a service come on by
To take my leaves away.
The fact is, raking satisfies;
Indeed, invigorates.
It really is good exercise
And not a task too great.
And so I do it every year
Before cold winter's call.
I rake and rake and haul and haul;
It's simply part of fall.

## Snake Escape

I sometimes find a garter snake
In the autumn when I rake
Taking off to quickly hide
In its slim skin and to glide
With a slither through the grass
Leaving leaves it leaves to pass
From the place where it's discovered
Until composure is recovered.
Only then it does its best
To lie low and take a rest,
Enough excitement for one day
Of feeling fright and much dismay,
Rather stressed by its mistake
In being found beneath my rake.

## Deck Leaves

Air currents on my deck keep blowing
Curled up leaves round and round
Till at last a few are falling
Over its edge to drop on down
To the ground far below
Twisting and turning as they fall
Onto my flagstone patio
Like they're paying a courtesy call
Before they scamper to my lawn
Slowed down by damp and waiting grass
Till much later they are gone
Moved by stronger winds that pass,
Tumbling then a few times more,
Until I rake, an endless chore!

## Leaves Keep Falling

Leaves keep falling, falling, falling.
I can hear them calling, calling:
"Come and rake us; quit your stalling!"
Which I find to be most galling.
"Rake yourselves!" I want to shout.
That's what fall should be about.
"Find a breeze, you leaves, and blow
Where you want to. Please, just go!"
Sadly, pleading does no good.
Leaves won't listen, never could.
None will leave, for goodness sake.
Might as well go out and rake.

## Leaves Gone But Not For Long

I've raked new leaves till I'm half dead
That drifted down and overspread
My lawn, and though for now they're gone,
I must suspect it's not for long.
I hope the winds that blow on high
Won't pick piled leaves up where they lie
To scatter back where they had been
So I must rake them once again.
I really feel at times like this
While raking I'm like Sisyphus.
Just when I think I'm done and stop,
The wind picks up and more leaves drop,
Alighting on my once clear yard.
Wish it was easy, not so hard.

## Time To Leave

Looking out, more maple leaves
Drop casually, but steady,
Float to the ground with every breeze
To join those raked already.

Fast as I try my grass to clear,
I'm left with no solution.
From heaven above more leaves appear
With random distribution.

"Stop!" I say, "Leave me alone;
Go yonder, winds that blow.
I beg of you, to parts unknown
Be gone, I say, just go!

"Leaves, honestly, is it so hard
To find another place?
Try landing in my neighbor's yard;
It has by far more space!"

But stubbornly these leaves won't move;
My pleading does no good.
No matter how much I reprove,
They don't do what they should.

And so I rake and rake and rake,
And rake and rake still more,
Hardly even take a break
Until my arms are sore.

"We've got you covered!" cry the leaves.
"We've got the drop on you!
Rake all you want—no one believes
Your work will soon be through.

"Rake day and night, work till you fall
Perspiring with exhaustion.
Even then that won't be all;
We leave you with this caution:

"Rake on, regardless, we'll be back;
Oh yes, we will, next year,
Ready for a new attack;
Of that you may be sure.

"So give it up, man, call it quits;
You may as well resign
Yourself to autumn's leafy tricks,
Our treat's by fall's design."

## Oak Leaves Hold On

In autumn, maple leaves catch fire
With colors bright we most admire,
And soon these leaves once green turn red
And yellow, orange, then all are shed

Below their branches all around
In layers scattered on the ground.
The oaks, more stubborn, keep their coats
All scalloped brown, as if to dote

On every leaf, slow to let go.
They often drop, most after snow
As if to say "We hope to stay
Until some far-off windy day.

"Go rake, or try to, if you can
The few leaves fallen, but our plan
Is slow and sure, like needled fir
That pine to keep their strong verdure,

"And much prefer to hold their own
Within their branches' skirted zone."
Meanwhile we rake and rake and rake
Until at last we take a break

To catch our breaths and look to where
Our maple trees once full are bare,
While every stingy leafy oak
Withholds its own as if to joke:

"You cannot have our leaves just yet.
Like cards we hold them close to chest
And play them slowly one by one
To see your raking's never done!"

# IX. Autumn Time

## Hummers Gone South

The hummingbirds have headed south
Abandoning our feeders
Enjoyed by every hungry mouth,
These tiny happy eaters.
We shall miss them every day
Till spring when they return.
Of course we knew they could not stay;
'Twas easy to discern,
Since now the days betray a chill
And fall is coming on.
Yet we know these creatures will
Remember, though they're gone,
Here they have a faithful friend
To welcome them back home again.

## Garden Harvest

The harvest comes in fall each year
When peppers, pumpkins, and squash appear
With vegetables of every sort
And berries by the pint and quart.
Fruit will weigh down apple trees,
Some as low as to their knees
That in the spring were full of blossoms
Pollinated by bees for autumn.
Gardens ripen and await
Picking with their numbers great,
An abundance they provide
To be sold here far and wide,
Enough to feed us all the year,
Gathered before winter's here.

## Cold and Rainy Weather

Rainy weather today we've got;
Pleasant outside it is not.
Worse than this I guess could be
Heat with high humidity,
Or cruel cold with snow and sleet
And slick ice upon our street.
Snowbirds do not brave this stuff;
They know when they've had enough.
But who are we here to complain
Just because of cold and rain
When we're warm at home inside,
Snug and dry, well occupied?
Really, there's no need to pout;
We can simply wait it out.

## Orange Twilight

The twilight sky was orange tonight,
A rare and unexpected sight;
To see the landscape bathed in color
Seemed surprising, unlike any other
We have ever seen before
At the lake and so much more,
Not faint at all, but rich and glowing,
Then finally departing, going
Into darkness, losing light,
Shadows growing long, a sight
That though its coming could not stay,
We'll remember how the play
Of light was magical to see,
And had you been here, you'd agree.

## One Fall Night

Lusters seen on sky and tree,
The moon out glowing peacefully,
Are visual music to the mind.
Delights of fall so dear to find:
The smell of clover sweet afield,
Stalks of corn aburst with yield.
Birds excited sense and know
It won't be long before they go
To places south, their leaving timed
Before the snow, to a warmer clime—
Like monarchs fly to Mexico,
Amazing they know where to go.
From these we gain serenity
In nature's true tranquility.

## Harvest Moon

The harvest moon glows bright and bold;
It is a marvel to behold.
The night is young, yet moon is old,
About it many stories told.
It rises in the evening sky
Adrift, like a balloon;
It seems to float and climb on high
Inspiring Claire de Lune.
For music of the eye is there
Though silent, without sounds.
It's placid, still we are aware
It moves and makes its rounds
Until night fades with morning light;
At dawn it passes from our sight.

## Time for Planting Tulips

The time for planting tulips
Is now or nearly gone.
Each night the temperature dips,
With November coming on.
Soon the soil will harden
Against the icy blast.
We'll place bulbs in the garden
Before the moment's passed
To provide them depth protection
Beneath the frozen ground
Here in their own small section
To be safe when frost comes 'round.
Our bulbs need planting deep
Before their winter's sleep.

## Goose Summer Gone

Goose summer once again comes round
With webs all gossamer*
In bushes and upon the ground
In autumn's finery fair.

Featherlike first winter snow
Will soon begin to blow
Teasing trees to drop last leaves
And let them fall below.

Frozen flakes of downy white
Will wing down from the sky,
Falling, floating, settling
In drifts of snow banked high.

Magical to art commence
Winds will sculpt and curve
Little swerves of snow by fence
Delightful to observe.

Later, draped in deep darkness
Beneath a cold moonlight,
Like petticoats or sparkly dress
They'll show their silvery white,

All serene, a lovely scene,
Icy, frozen, still,
Covering a lawn once green
As only winter will.

-------------------------------
*The word gossamer, from the Middle English gossomer,
 is from "goose summer," the brief summer-like warm-up
 in late autumn that lasts a few days before the frost comes
 in, when filmy web-like threads float in the air, and plentiful
 geese are in season, pausing to enjoy the warmth on their way
 southward. "Gossamer.," N. p.810. (1971). In *The Compact Edition
 of the Oxford English Dictionary* , Oxford: Oxford University Press.

## Geese Migration

Geese migrating out of mist
Take to autumn air.
Instinct they cannot resist
Is saying go elsewhere.

Graceful, they are soon aloft
Lifting with their wings
Upward through a cloudy froth
The morning's vapor brings,

Streaming up, low then high,
Steady in their course,
Heading south, winter-shy,
Abandoning the north,

In the distance turning, winging,
Excited, underway,
Knowing somehow where they're going
In wave on wave array

Till we hear them only faintly,
Distant in their cry,
In joyful voice, almost quaintly,
As they pass on by.

## Cardinal Plans

I've watched a cardinal flit in trees,
Sit and survey earth with ease,
And I've wondered, does he know
Fall is here and with it snow
Soon will float down through the air
With a drop in temperature?
Does he worry, does he care?
Does he have plans to prepare?
Winter will be here all right,
Freezing cold day and night.
Will this bird be taking flight
Or will he stay and be all right,
Just resigned or brave and bold
To persevere through the cold?

## Hints of Winter

When hints of winter turn nights cold,
And winds start blowing harsh and bold,
Dashing round with frosty bluster,
Forcing trees their strength to muster
Against fierce gusts that bend their boughs
To such degree as each allows,
Thrashing leaves until near all
Give up their grasp, let go, and fall,
And geese out floating on the pond
Begin to call "time to move on,"
It's then we know it won't be long
Till autumn, too, will soon be gone.

## How Autumn Leaves

When autumn leaves once again,
Clouds will mount and bring us rain.
Winds will bluster, blow and batter,
Branches shake, their leaves to scatter,

But first they'll dazzle every eye
With rich arrays and hues on high,
As burdened branches start to thin
And winter signs start sneaking in.

A sudden chill will fill the air
And frost will soon be everywhere
Like crystalline glue to hold leaves down
And blanket lawns all over town.

Geese in streams will take their flight
Happy, honking in our sight,
Nights grow colder and we'll know
They foreshadow coming snow.

Then one day, when dawn awakes,
We'll rise and open wide our drapes
And by our windows raptly stand
To view a snowy wonderland.

# X. Winter Wonders

## Before the Snow

Time to leave, we need to go
Home; the forecast calls for snow,
Tons expected storming down,
Enough to inundate our town
With wind ferocious set to blow
And temperatures to five below.
Drifting slopes and snow banks steep
Could reach, perhaps, up to two feet
Beginning here this afternoon.
We need to hunker down and soon,
Get ready to weather this massive storm
Till it ends tomorrow morn
When digging out we'll need a hand
To cope with a blizzard wonderland.

## First Snow

The night grew cold and overhead
A storm was brewing, the forecast said,
Fed by fronts of arctic air
With snow and dropping temperature.

We went to bed, dozed off to sleep
Expecting snow would fall and deep,
Slept soundly as a grizzly bear
In peaceful dreams without a care.

Next morning, early we arose,
Hurriedly put on our clothes,
Wondering what we would find
Outside. We opened drapes and blinds

To behold what would astound:
Snow-drift sculptures all around,
Forms to marvel at, each tree
A magic frozen fantasy.

The night had left its cold surprise:
Our lake turned stone, snow over ice
With surface covered white as chalk;
We thought it must be hard as rock.

We ate our breakfast on the double,
Bundled up to go and shovel,
Quickly donned our warm snow suits,
Shoved our shoes into our boots,

Opened our snow-drifted door,
Felt the cold, with more in store,
Pulled on our gloves, put hats on heads
Half-wishing we were snug in beds!

The snow had stopped and now a breeze
Was gently blowing through the trees.
Limbs stretched out were all but still
With heavy snow, each held its fill.

With shovels then we went to work
To clear our sidewalk, toss and jerk,
Throwing snow into the air
To clear a pathway to our stair.

Then the driveway—what a job!
Shovelfuls we had to lob
Away from where the plow went through:
An extra snow bank left to do.

Finally finished, we trudged inside,
Spread our mittens so they dried,
Warmed up, drank a chocolate brew,
Refreshment for our little crew.

That's what we did when winter came;
Still do today, it's much the same
Digging out from loads of snow.
It's kind of fun.... Well, *we* think so!

## Snowflakes Dancing

Snowflakes dancing grace the air
Like Ginger did with Fred Astaire
In pirouettes as fine and fair
As once these two were debonair,
Waltzing all across the sky,
Skittering from clouds on high,
Twirling in a winsome way
With abandon through the day,
Gliding, sliding with the wind,
Promenading out and in,
Floating like an evening gown,
Smooth as silk down to the ground,
Whirling lightly on the breeze.
We love winter days like these.

## No Snow Woe

It snowed last night and continues now;
My driveway's blocked until a plow
Comes here to clear the snow away
Whenever that might be today,
Which means for now I'll have to wait,
Trapped in my house and contemplate
The winter white all 'round I see
That nature's grace has given me.
It's quiet here, not much to do,
Except to wait an hour or two.
While snow is gusting in a flurry,
I'll just relax, no need to hurry,
Nor to worry; it's nice to rest
And just enjoy the season's best.

## Winter Weather

The temperature outside is low
To match our house hugged deep in snow
That fell twelve inches yesterday
And with the cold will likely stay.
Accordingly, my bones have felt
It isn't likely soon to melt.
I'm saying this because I find
When snow falls down it does not mind
What forecasters say on TV
With claims of predictability,
Indeed, assuring accuracy
With near infallibility.
The snow is simply not aware
What others say and does not care.

## At 10 Below

With wind chill here near 10 below,
My driveway's drifted in with snow.
It's not the kind of day I like
Considering dangers like frostbite.
I don't go out on days like this;
It's just too cold to take that risk.
Instead I stay in, hunkered down
Like everybody else in town.
The river here, a sight to see,
Is frozen over solidly,
With Canada geese nowhere in sight.
When it's this cold they all take flight.
Where they go, I have no clue,
But if I were them, I'd be gone, too!

## River Ice

River ice that I can see
Extends downstream for miles from me,
Stretching to the distant shore
Atop the water where before
December it did not exist
When warm enough to ice resist.
Ice now has grown to inches thick
And plans to stay, in fact to stick
Around for maybe two more months
Where open water showed there once.
Now locked, it won't go anywhere
Until the weather warms, turns fair,
After which we're sure to see
The ice disperse, though gradually.

## Not Too Cold

I do not like the cold
I admit, although
If the truth be told
I do enjoy the snow,
The look of it at least
When watching warm inside
As flakes like leaves released
From trees fall down and glide
So playfully when wind
Dashes all around,
Laying layers thin,
Or deeper on the ground.
Cold I do not like,
But snow is a delight.

## On Our Snowy Street

How deep the snow that fell last night
Has covered up my yard in white.
Two feet have fallen, maybe more,
Enough to block my red front door.
The contrast is a sight to see,
The door and sidewalk pleasantly
Adding color to our street,
A cheery sight as if to greet
The daring few who may pass by
Wearing boots in snow this high
To walk their dogs, as many do,
Before the plows have yet come through.
Their dogs are romping through the snow
Along the sidewalks as they go.

## Plow's Been Through

The plow's been through
What can I do?
It's left its little gift
And so snow bank—
With plow to thank—
I get to shovel it,

To push and scrape,
To hold and lift,
To break my poor sore back,
And if I'm not too careful, well
I'll have a heart attack!

Oh, yes, I know
The snow must go,
The plow must plod along,
But leaving me its pile of snow
And ice just still seems wrong!

I think it best
Not to protest,
But do you get my drift?
To plow, while well-intended
I say, "Spare me this, your gift!"

## Leaves Waft and Wander

Leaves waft and wander
Through the air.
It's winter;
Why are they still there
When the ground is all around
Frozen solid, clearly bound
Up in winter's lengthy sleep,
While the snow is crusty, deep?
Why must these leaves be moving now
With the wind that will allow
More and more of leafy clutter
To accumulate and flutter
Across our snowy yard at will,
Carefree, lackadaisical?

## Snowy Day

Morning brings a gray-veiled sun
And soon a heavy snow's begun.
Flakes come floating from the sky,
Whirling, swirling till they lie

Softly resting white on white.
Like a feather fog, they light
Deep and deeper, without sound,
Drifting catawampus down,

Falling with a billion flakes
Banking streets and frozen lakes,
Dusting over hedge and tree
So thick some forms we hardly see

With little melting, crisp and cold—
Making new what once looked old—
Painting every shrub and fence
With a brightness fresh and dense.

Now a cardinal makes a show—
Stunning— out our front window,
Causing clumps of snow to fall,
Hunting berries near a wall.

How the birches bend and blend
Into the landscape, and the end
Of every street is covered in white;
What a marvel and delight!

We go out in its aftermath
With our task to clear a path,
Shovel out and briefly play
At snowball fights along the way.

Soon the neighbor kids turn out
In quilted snowsuits, walk about
With excitement and a plan
To make a jolly tall snowman.

Sure enough! They build him high,
Add carrot nose and coal, each eye,
With a scarf wrapped 'round his neck
And a corncob pipe just for effect.

He's built to tower up six feet
Facing toward our unplowed street.
"How do you do?" He seems to say
To folks out walking dogs our way.

We go inside but the next day
A snowplow passes our driveway
Throwing forth an icy mound
Rising three feet from the ground.

Out we have to go again
To clear it off as best we can.
Then it's back inside to stay
Warm with chocolate drinks, and play

Board games spread out on the floor—
Away from drafts, not near the door.
All's well within our homey world;
We're warm as cats content and curled.

Just listen, all's serene outside,
A peaceful landscape far and wide.
Let snow come when and where it may
To make great memories of this day
That ever in our minds will stay,
Good times and beauty winter's way.

## Squirrel Tracks in Snow

The ground is frozen here today
And for more months will likely stay
So that squirrels will find it hard
To dig up acorns in our yard
Buried so they do not show
Where these critters need to go
For their meals sought at their leisure,
Seeking out this hidden treasure
Held within their memory,
Though through snow they cannot see
Where they put this sustenance
Without much hint or evidence.
Their tracks in snow crisscross our lawn
As their hopeful search goes on.

## Meditation on Snow

In the folds of fallen snow
And the banks that drift and blow,
In the icy shaking leaves
And the glassy-coated trees
Is a splendor winter brings,
Precious in these natural things.
Then what springs into the mind
Is the glory that we find
When we pause to take a look
To see the care that nature took,
And to marvel feeling awe
At this beauty till its thaw,
A wonder that this could be so,
A lovely gift wrapped up in snow.

## Snowy Magic

One winter morning still as night,
Cavernous dark yet wondrous white,
I trudged alone with canvas pack
Down Main Street toward our paper shack.

Not a soul moved anywhere,
Not one car, none were there;
But I, a boy, had ventured out
Early for my paper route.

Snow was floating in the air,
Dancing, drifting everywhere,
Light as lilting angel hair,
White and soft, fine and fair,

Glittering and gossamer,
Shadowed here and sparkling there,
Forming patterns strange and rare
Like magic castles built on air.

The county courthouse on my right
Stood fanciful, snow-outlined, bright,
As half asleep I tramped on slow
Past glimmering streetlights dimmed by snow.

I felt the wind enough to shiver,
Intent to do my job: deliver
Sunday news for a waiting world
While all around the snow storm swirled,

Blew against my parka coat
With wool scarf tucked to shield my throat.
The shack, though spare, was brightly lit,
Smelled of newsprint as I entered it,

Papers bundled by the door
Ready to lift up off the floor,
Break apart, count and stuff
Into my pack, just enough.

Soon bagged, I flung them over my shoulder
And started rounds as winds blew colder,
Snow drifts deepened, moon shown brighter.
Each paper delivered made my pack lighter

Taking them to each customer
Exactly where they would prefer.
At last the wind blew less, diminished
As my task I finally finished.

Tired but happy, I headed home,
Work completed all on my own,
Satisfied with what I'd done
Accomplishing what I'd begun.

That wintry dawn is now long gone,
My life, of course, much changed, moved on,
Yet still and fondly I remember
The snowy magic of that white December.

## Winter Morning

The dawn reveals a changing sky:
Orange fades to pink then gradually
Through the branches of our trees
Shadows dampen by degrees,
And distant hills lie low, sublime.
Winter feels like frozen time.
Saplings covered to their knees
Are buried in the snow's deep freeze.
Birds are silent, squirrels asleep;
Most activity can keep.
On days like this it just seems best
To hunker down and let things rest.
One month more or two will bring
Waking days that signal spring.

# XI. Winter Into Spring Again

## Waiting Out Winter

Waiting out winter
With its last arctic blast,
We wish for warmer weather
With cold days gone past.
We stand by our window
And hopeful look out
For more sun to show,
Though this is in doubt,
Wishing for days
Milder to come
While winter delays
Here today, not quite done.
We look for the spring
That tomorrow may bring.

## Bird Tracks

Across the snow new tracks we see
Of little birds whose feet are wee.
They barely even make a scratch,
A cardinal maybe, or nuthatch,
Imprints delicate and narrow,
Possibly an English sparrow,
One short inch in length at most,
Hardly there, light as a ghost,
White on white with slightest shadow
From brief touchdown, and then skedaddle,
Gone from ground back into air.
We'd hardly know a bird was there
Except to see these little hints:
Tiny feather-light snowprints.

## Think Summer!

When winter seems a bummer,
Forget it and think summer!
Sunshine drenching all day long,
Grass blades greening on your lawn,
Songs of birds everywhere
Twittering their happy share,
Bees a-buzzing, breezes light,
Lightning bugs that blink at night,
Walks with just a jacket on,
Happy that the cold is gone,
Water flowing, no more ice,
A sandy beach where swimming's nice,
Picnic afternoons till dark
To warm the heart at a park.
When all of this I bring to mind,
It's like winter's gone, left far behind.

## Glistening Branches

Icy branches glow and glisten
As sunlight strikes them; come and listen.
Now and then we hear "kerplop"
As melting ice begins to drop
From coated trees; it's falling down
Making that amusing sound.
On the ground the snow is wet
Where animals, their feet have set
Like Hollywood where stars all went
To press their feet in wet cement.
New tracks crisscross from tree to tree;
Their paths from here are clear to see.
Yet soon all this will melt away,
Nature's drama, winter's play.

## The Sun Is Beaming

Sunbeams branch in bright array
With days grown longer, spring on its way.
Deep snow's receding on fields today
And though it's March, cold cannot stay.
The back of winter seems broken, though
We still of course could get more snow
As we march toward April, this we know:
Cool winds can linger and well may blow.
Today, however, we'd like to think
Warm weather's closer, near the brink.
The sun shines higher, slower to sink
With golden fire to turn clouds pink.
Good-bye cold weather! Sun, come and play!
Bring melting warmth to chase snow away!

## Melting Snowman

Mister snowman, melting, melting,
Feels that warmer days have come
With the bright sun rays compelling,
Telling him cold winter's done.
Now his eyes of coal are missing
And he's lost his carrot nose.
Stick arms gradually are bending,
Neck collapsing in the throes
Of decline with fading winter,
Giving rise to springtime heat,
Telling snowman in the hinter-
Land he soon will meet defeat
As his body in a muddle
Turns into a water puddle.

## Warmer Days Ahead

The morning snow that came
Today is melted, gone,
Hurried off by rain
From resting trees and lawn.
Soon enough the spring
Will finish off old ice
And warmer days will bring
Flowers, ours to prize,
Rising with the sun,
Dancing in its glow
With longer hours begun.
Then greenery will show
And blossoms we will see
In all their finery.

# The Quiet Crocus

The crocus pokes through frosty ground
So quietly it makes no sound,
At least that you or I can hear,
Not even if we cup our ear
To listen with the greatest care,
And yet it moves, arising where
It is intent to grow and knows
How to emerge in spite of snows
That more than likely soon will melt.
When spring winds blow, rain comes to pelt
The ground around it, cold and yet
More than welcome, bringing wet
To dampen earth and slowly sink,
A windfall thirsty roots can drink.
Then crocus blooms greet warming sun
Bringing joy to everyone.

## Leaf Gathering

The tumultuous winds of early spring
Bring to the earth an offering:
Oak leaves that clung all winter long
To stubborn branches, still not gone,
Finally past winter snow
Are at last dislodged, let go,
Falling fast with raucous rain,
Dashing to our lawn again,
Blown and scattered on the grass,
Lying all about en masse.
Like in the fall they'll soon partake
Of our gathering by rake.

## The Gift

A miracle it is, by far
That we exist and simply are
Able to observe it's so,
This, and that we even know
A world around us moves and grows
From galaxies to layered rose,
That after night we find a morn
Where plants can flower and seeds are borne
Aloft into the stuff of air,
That beauty lives in nature's care,
That light is processed by our eyes
And we've come to realize
The universe in which we drift
Is wondrous, a stupendous gift.

## Waiting for Daffodils

We wait for daffodils
To rise up from the ground
Beyond our windowsills
Where sleeping bulbs are found.
They hide beneath the snow
Portending yellow color,
Soon to up and show
Their pedigree a-flower.
Brief will be their stay
Buffeted by wind,
Late April into May,
After they begin,
As cheerfully they bring
Their blooming message: spring!

## Spring Morning

Light streams through my window
Too bright for me to see,
Brilliant in its glow,
Yet pleasant, warming me.
It's morning in the spring—
My daffodils are out.
Birds fly and swoop and sing
With hungry chicks about.
It is that time of year
When leaves are turning green,
Azure skies dawn clear,
A truly lovely scene,
When all about me thrive—
It's good to be alive.

# XII. The March of Time

# The March of Time

The March of time advances here,
A sign that April must be near,
And May will follow rather soon
To bring fresh spring on into June.
July will warm and August next,
Then September's fall effects.
October waiting in the wings
Hints cooler weather November brings.
Thence December snows to bury
Us, but welcome January,
Till February, freezing, harsh,
Returns us to—full circle—March;
Thus goes 'round the calendar year,
The annual dance of seasons here.

# About the Author

Jeffry Glover, winner of a Robert Frost Foundation poetry award and a top ten Outstanding Leader in Education award, creates delightful rhyming poems for all ages. He draws upon his experience as a language arts teacher, school librarian, and library games inventor to produce tales in verse that are in turn whimsical and witty, humorous and heart-warming, and just plain fun to read, especially aloud. His work as a library promotion specialist reached millions of children and adults around the world to encourage reading and the discovery and exploration of library resources. In retirement Jeff has begun publishing his poetry and is the author of over 8,000 sonnets along with many other poems on a wide range of topics. Jeffry and his spouse live near the river shore along with sandhill cranes, hummingbirds, and Baltimore orioles. His books of verse include *9 Lively Cat Tales and Other Pet Poems*, *The Wildebeest and a Bunch of Crock and Other Animal Story Poems*, and more entertaining adventures in rhyme. Visit PoemsforPleasurePress.com, or scan the QR code below to check out Jeff's books!

www.ingramcontent.com/pod-product-compliance
Ingram Content Group UK Ltd.
Pitfield, Milton Keynes, MK11 3LW, UK
UKHW041817110325
456069UK00001B/94